D1710828

CREEPING SLIME

SLIME MOLDS

by Ellen Lawrence

Consultant:
Mark Fricker
Associate Professor, Department of Plant Sciences
University of Oxford
United Kingdom

BEARPORT PUBLISHING

New York, New York

Credits

Cover, © ImageBroker/Alamy; 4L, © Matauw/Dreamstime; 4R, © dugdax/Shutterstock; 5, © ImageBroker/Alamy; 6, © Ruth Owen Books; 7, © Eye of Science/Science Photo Library; 8, © Ruth Owen Books; 9, © Alex Hyde/Nature Picture Library; 10TL, © Naturepix/Alamy; 10TR, © Ivan Marjanovic/Shutterstock; 10B, © Johannes Menge/Shutterstock; 11, © blickwinkel/Alamy; 12, © Gillian Pullinger/Alamy; 13, © Premaphotos/Alamy; 14, © Frank Hecker/Alamy; 15, © Sabena Jane Blackbird/Alamy; 16, © Alex Hyde/Nature Picture Library; 17, © Eye of Science/Science Photo Library; 18, © François Peaudecerf, Gabriel Amselem, and Karen Alim; 19, © Bearport Publishing; 20T, © Alex Hyde/Nature Picture Library; 20B, © Eye of Science/Science Photo Library; 21, © Simia Attentive/Shutterstock; 22L, © Lamyai/Shutterstock; 22TR, © fullempty/Shutterstock; 22BR, © Ruth Owen Books; 23TL, © Eye of Science/Science Photo Library; 23TC, © Lotus Studio/Shutterstock; 23TR, © nobeastsofierce/Shutterstock; 23BL, © bob.leccinum.Robert Kozak/Shutterstock; 23BC, © Pressmaster/Shutterstock; 23BR, © Dr. Morley Read/Shutterstock.

Publisher: Kenn Goin
Senior Editor: Joyce Tavolacci
Creative Director: Spencer Brinker
Photo Researcher: Ruth Owen Books

Library of Congress Cataloging-in-Publication Data

Names: Lawrence, Ellen, 1967– author.
Title: Creeping slime : slime molds / by Ellen Lawrence.
Description: New York, New York : Bearport Publishing, [2019] | Series:
   Slime-inators & other slippery tricksters | Includes
   bibliographical references and index.
Identifiers: LCCN 2018016359 (print) | LCCN 2018020351 (ebook) |
   ISBN 9781642800616 (ebook) | ISBN 9781642800609 (library)
Subjects: LCSH: Myxomycetes—Juvenile literature.
Classification: LCC QK635 (ebook) | LCC QK635 .L39 2019 (print) |
   DDC 579.5/2—dc23
LC record available at https://lccn.loc.gov/2018016359

For more information, write to Bearport Publishing Company, Inc., 45 West 21st Street, Suite 3B, New York, New York 10010. Printed in the United States of America.

10 9 8 7 6 5 4 3 2 1

Contents

A Hungry Blob

In a dark, damp forest, something slimy is oozing over a rotting log.

Long, slippery strands stretch in every direction.

The bright yellow goo is slime mold.

It looks like a blob, but it's actually a living thing— and it's hungry!

slime mold

a damp forest

slime mold

Slime molds are not actually molds, as scientists once thought. They belong to a group of living things called myxomycetes (mik-soh-MY-seetz).

5

A Tiny Amoeba

A slime mold doesn't begin life as a big, gooey blob.

It starts out as a tiny **amoeba**.

Some living things, such as animals and plants, are made up of billions of **cells**.

A slime mold amoeba is just a single cell!

It's so small that it can only be seen under a **microscope**.

a drawing of a slime mold amoeba

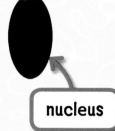

nucleus

An amoeba has no brain, but it does have a nucleus (NOO-klee-uhss). The nucleus is like the amoeba's control center.

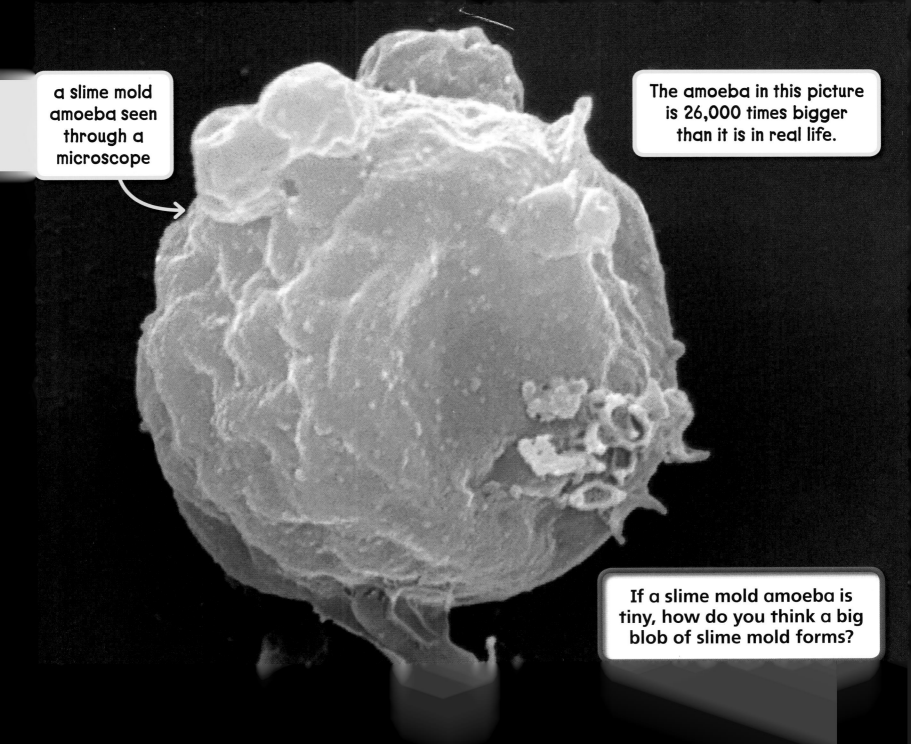

Supersize Slime Mold

A slime mold amoeba searches for food in the soil where it lives.

If it finds food, it grows bigger. How?

The amoeba's nucleus divides in two, allowing the cell to grow.

This happens again and again until the amoeba becomes a slimy blob—or super cell.

At this stage, the blob is known as plasmodial (plaz-MOH-dee-uhl) slime.

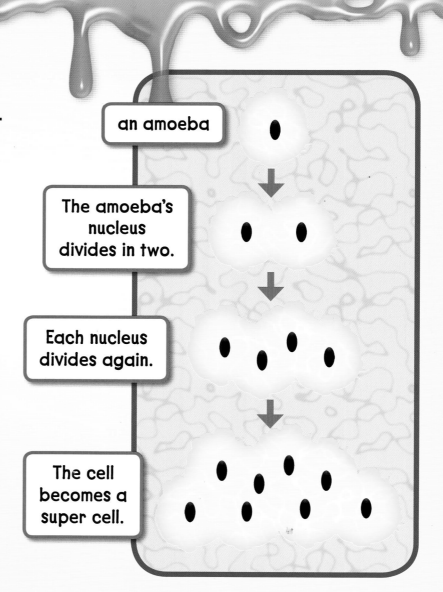

an amoeba

The amoeba's nucleus divides in two.

Each nucleus divides again.

The cell becomes a super cell.

A mass of slime mold can be less than half an inch (1.27 cm) thick. However, it can grow large enough to cover a car!

Colors and Shapes

There are about 900 different kinds of slime molds.

They come in many different colors and strange shapes.

The false puffball slime mold got its name because it looks like a puffball mushroom.

The scrambled egg slime mold is bright yellow and fluffy.

It also has another name—dog vomit slime mold!

false puffball slime mold

puffball mushroom

scrambled egg slime mold

Slime molds come in almost every color, except green. That's because slime molds don't contain chlorophyll (KLAWR-uh-fil). Chlorophyll is the substance that makes plants green and helps them create food.

This slime mold is named after its shape. What do you think it's called?
(The answer is on page 24.)

Slime molds are found in almost every part of the world.

They make their homes in forests, parks, and gardens.

They ooze over rotting leaves and logs.

A slime mold prefers to live where it's cool, damp, and dark.

This helps keep the slimy mass soft and gooey.

What do you think slime molds feed on?

wolf's milk slime mold on a tree trunk

If the weather gets too dry, a slime mold can become a hard, crusty lump called a sclerotium (skluh-ROH-shee-uhm). It can survive like this for years. Once it rains, the lump soaks up water and becomes soft and squishy again.

slime mold growing on a damp, mossy log

Suppertime!

A blob of slime mold feeds on **fungi** and **bacteria**, which grow on dead plants.

The blob has no mouth or stomach, so how does it eat?

A slime mold oozes over its food, completely covering its meal.

Next, it releases special substances onto the food to break it down.

Then, the slime mold soaks up **nutrients** directly from the food.

slime mold oozing over dead wood

Slime molds are part of nature's cleanup crew. As they feed, they help to break down dead plants and fungi.

yellow slime mold feeding on a dead mushroom

On the Hunt

How does a mass of slime with no brain find food?

As a slime mold searches for a meal, branchlike tendrils spread out from the slimy mass.

If a tendril discovers some food in a certain spot, it sends a message through the blob.

Then, more of the slime oozes to that spot to feed.

A slime mold can have hundreds of tendrils!

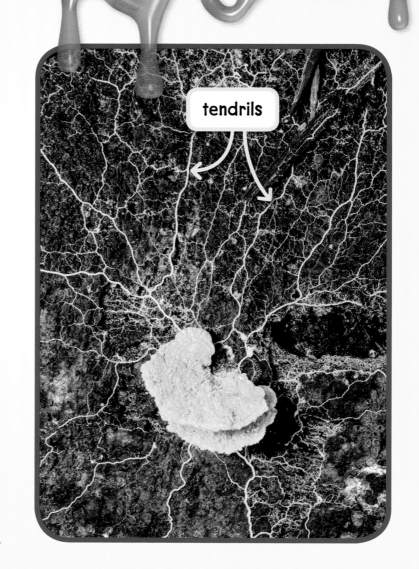

tendrils

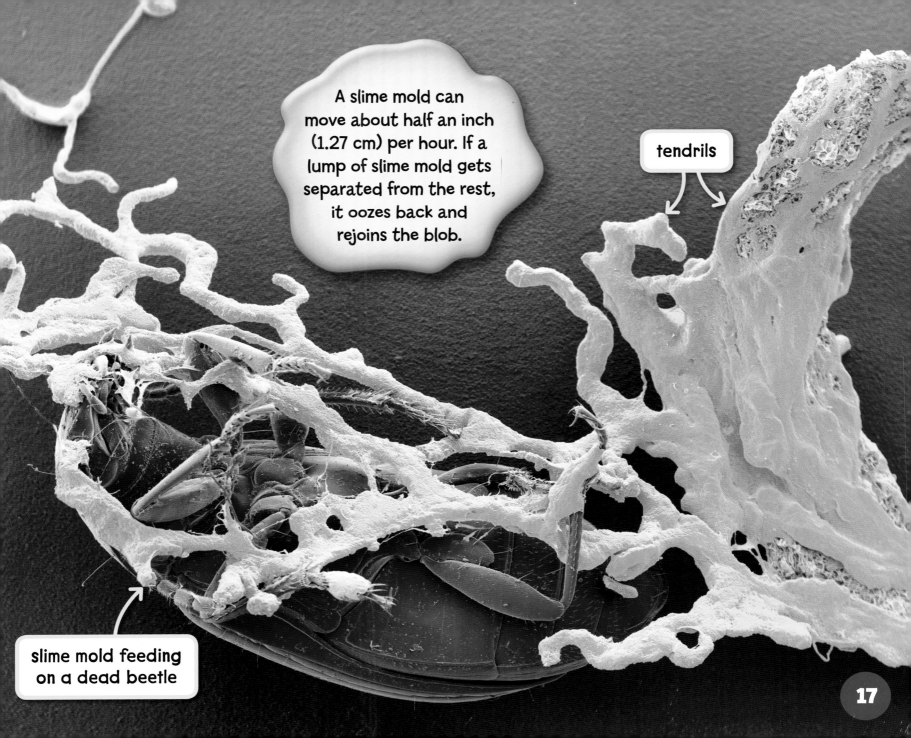

A slime mold can move about half an inch (1.27 cm) per hour. If a lump of slime mold gets separated from the rest, it oozes back and rejoins the blob.

tendrils

slime mold feeding on a dead beetle

Problem-Solving Slime

Scientists tested slime mold to discover if it could find food in a maze.

The slime mold's tendrils spread out, searching along the maze's passages.

When a tendril found a snack, the message was passed through the slime.

Then, all the tendrils headed to the food.

The slimy tendrils even found the shortest route to the meal!

slime mold solving a maze

Scientists discovered that the tendrils left a slimy trail as they moved through the maze. This trail told other tendrils that a passage had already been explored.

Slime Tracks Experiment

Can slime mold find the shortest routes between popular places on a map of Tokyo, Japan? Scientists conducted this experiment to find out.

1. A map of the area around Tokyo was used to set up the experiment.

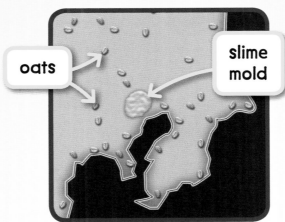

oats

slime mold

2. Oats were put on popular places on the map. Then, a blob of slime mold was placed on Tokyo.

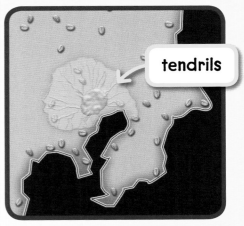

tendrils

3. The slime mold's tendrils spread out to find the food.

4. The tendrils covered the map in search of the oats.

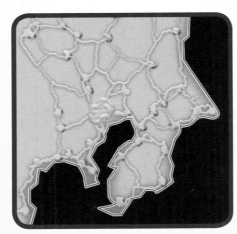

5. After about 26 hours, only the tendrils with the shortest paths to the food remained.

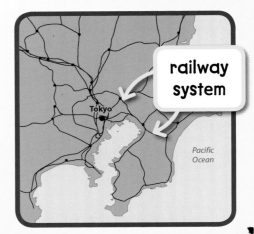

railway system

6. The pattern of the tendrils closely matched the railway system around Tokyo!

Making New Slime

If a slime mold cannot find enough food, it undergoes a big change.

Stalks tipped with tiny fruitlike blobs grow from the slimy mass.

Inside each fruit are millions of microscopic seedlike parts called spores.

When the fruits burst open, the spores are scattered.

One day, each tiny spore will become a slime mold amoeba!

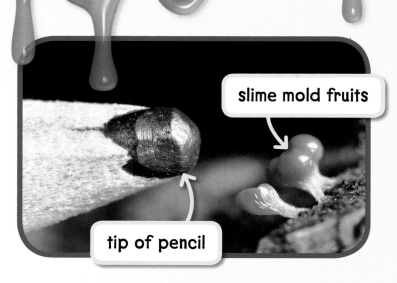

slime mold fruits

tip of pencil

spores

Science Lab

Make Slime Mold!

Mix up a batch of yellow slime and present a slime mold show-and-tell.

I. In a bowl, mix together the white glue and baking soda with a spoon.

2. Add several drops of yellow food coloring to the bowl and mix well. To make scrambled egg slime, mix in some foam balls.

foam balls

3. Add the contact lens solution to the mixture. Keep stirring until slime begins to form.

4. Take the slime out of the bowl and knead it with your hands until the slime has fully formed.

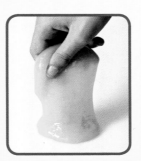

You will need:

- A bowl
- 4 fluid ounces of white glue
- ½ tablespoon of baking soda
- A spoon
- Yellow food coloring
- I cup of yellow foam balls (optional)
- I tablespoon of contact lens solution

Slime Mold Show-and-Tell

Use your slime to tell your friends and family about slime mold. Think about answering these questions during your presentation.

- **What is slime mold?**
- **How does slime mold find food?**
- **What happens if some slime mold is separated from the main blob?**

Science Words

amoeba (uh-MEE-buh) a living thing made up of just one cell

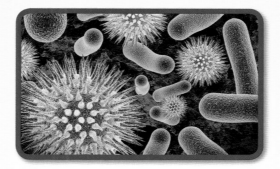

bacteria (bak-TEER-ee-uh) tiny living things; some bacteria are helpful while others cause disease

cells (SELZ) very tiny parts of a person, animal, plant, or other living thing

fungi (FUHN-jye) living things that include mushrooms

microscope (MYE-kruh-skope) a tool or machine used to see things that are too small to see with the eyes alone

nutrients (NOO-tree-uhnts) substances found in food needed by living things to stay healthy

23

Index

Read More

McDonald, Megan. *Stink and the Attack of the Slime Mold.* Somerville, MA: Candlewick Press (2016).

Riehecky, Janet. *Slime, Poop, and Other Wacky Animal Defenses (Blazers).* North Mankato, MN: Capstone (2012).

Shores, Lori. *How to Make Slime: A 4D Book (Pebble Plus).* North Mankato, MN: Capstone (2018).

Learn More Online

To learn more about slime molds, visit
www.bearportpublishing.com/Slime-inators

About the Author

Ellen Lawrence lives in the United Kingdom. Her favorite books to write are those about nature and animals. In fact, the first book Ellen bought for herself when she was six years old was the story of a gorilla named Patty Cake that was born in New York's Central Park Zoo.

Answer for Page 11

Because of its twisty shape and brown color, this slime mold is known as pretzel slime mold. It grows on dead wood.